CARLTON CHAMBER'S GUIDE TO MEETINGS

Wright and Reid Guides

wrightandreid.com

January, 2024

CONTENTS / AGENDA

Chapter 11

FEEDBACK AND EVALUATION

GLOSSARY

FURTHER READING AND ONLINE RESOURCES

INTRODUCTION

I trust you are sitting comfortably. Allow me to introduce myself. My name is Carlton Chambers. As someone who has been active in community service for around thirty years, I've been involved in meetings (both formal and informal) for many years. This book assists you with the subject, not just about the theory, it has plenty of practical advice based on my wide experience.

There are many types of meetings. We will look at the different ones later, with advice for meetings and tips for specific kinds of meetings.

You can even treat this book as a series of meetings between yourself (the student) and myself (the author). The agenda being the contents listed before this introduction. The venue is wherever you take this book.

And, if you wish, you can make appointments in your diary to read specific chapters of this book.

Those who wish to get more from meetings are the target audience for this book. You might find that you already know some of the stuff. I hope, however, there is plenty of information you find useful.

I will start by explaining the meaning of the meetings, why structure and purpose are important. After that, we explore different types.

When we have covered the basics, we look at the components of an effective meeting. After which, we examine the two most important components of meetings: yourself and other people. We then turn to the key roles of the chairperson (chair), secretary or facilitator and treasurer, and we cover key documents such as the agenda, minutes and financial reports (where required.)

The beginning of the book builds up to an important chapter for you. Chapter 4 is important as it is about you being effective. I'll show you how to stand out, to be in control, and how to avoid feeling unimportant. Although most people are helpful, there could be others who are mischievous. Throughout the process, I'll be using my experience to show you how to avoid the traps that others set.

At the end of the book, we discuss the important annual meeting, why all meetings should end with feedback, and there's a helpful glossary.

No matter what type your meetings are, what kind of organisation yours is and what the purposes of your meetings are, I hope you find the advice given useful and interesting.

Please prepare for this book as you should for all your meetings. Take a pen and notebook with you to record key points, ideas, and reminders that come to mind. Indeed, here's some advice: have two pens with you in case the first one runs out of ink or gets borrowed and not returned.

It also helps you to become a hero when you offer a pen to someone who has forgotten theirs.

Regards,

Carlton Chambers

Chapter 1

THE PURPOSE OF MEETINGS

A meeting is not usually an isolated event. Often it is part of an ongoing process. Two questions you should ask now: What is the meeting's purpose? Is it worth setting up the meeting or attending?

Not just an isolated event, a meeting is usually an important part of a sequence of actions designed to reach one or more specific goals. A meeting is a success where it ends with a clear picture of the actions needed next.

Where people come together to have a chat, where the gathering ends making no changes or plans, we have a social event. A gathering where people say their views and less than half an hour later forget what they said is also a social event. Neither are meetings with a purpose.

Each year a record of attendance at meetings was published. The press used the numbers to create a league table. This was not fair to the attendees as they all could not attend every meeting, especially those who were not invited to every meeting or who had a clash of meetings.

One attendee, who came low in the league table, told the public that meetings were a waste of time and he'd rather be doing something else. He achieved little.

While many might agree with him, in my experience this is not true. While I have been in a few meetings where I wondered what is the point of attending, most meetings are productive and enlightening.

Consider meeting outcomes. Examine how they benefit the overall purpose and each member. Be aware that others might use the meeting for their own personal outcomes. They may have a hidden agenda.

Each meeting presents opportunities for you to promote your image and is an excellent opportunity for networking.

Arrive early or leave late. This is beneficial for networking and getting assistance. Carry some of your business cards with you, as well as a handy notebook and pen.

Arriving early at a new venue provides a chance to explore. Setting off to the venue early is also a good idea just in case you encounter major road works, bus delays, or the car park is full.

A colleague was well known for being late, which she did deliberately as she believed it showed how important she was. It didn't. The meeting started on time anyway. She also liked to get her photograph on social media. She arranged for a popular blogger to take a picture of the small group for his blog. When she eventually got to the meeting, late as usual, she became angry because the photographer had not waited for her and took the picture without her. This is one reason why it is important to arrive in good time.

Where the meeting is held is important. While it is usually useful to have the meeting in the regular location, sometimes it's helpful to hold it somewhere else.

This is handy where there is a need to reach out to certain people or for participants to visit a place that is a subject of the meeting.

A supermarket chain wanted to build a new store in a residential area. The board held a public meeting in a nearby hall. This helped the members to become familiar with the area, as well as the locals appreciating not having to travel far from their homes.

Back to the concept of hidden agenda. Try understand why other participants are there.

It could be to enhance their CV. This can be useful as they wish to make a useful impression.

Or is it simply their manager asked them to attend? Is it to avoid other work? In these cases,

consider if it is useful that they attend. They can be motivated given the right inspiration.

Look for ways such as delegating tasks to encourage them to join in.

Do not invite them if their presence is pointless. Most times, you will be doing them a favour

by not wasting their time.

A meeting called just to show people that something is being done with no intention of

achieving anything is a waste of your time and of others.

Beware of those with hidden agendas to appear more important. If it helps the process, that's

fine. However, if their purpose is to appear smart with little or no commitment to the process,

that person could become disruptive no matter how nice they seem. To counter this, the other

participants should remain focused.

If two or more of these people are present, a conflict may disrupt the meeting. In that case, it's

crucial for everyone to keep focused, or exclude the egotists to remove the disruption.

If there is someone whose attendance is vital, schedule the meeting for when they can attend.

I recall one public meeting held by objectors who complained that the developers did not

show. It turned out the developers were not consulted on whether or not they would be able

to attend at that time, and having little time to prepare could not attend.

It is worth reminding what the key purpose of a meeting is: to be part of a process that works

towards desired goals. That is why future action points should be the key results of meetings.

There is another key purpose just as important, although it rarely appears as an agenda item. To energise and motivate participants. You can nurture enthusiasm by letting participants understand others appreciate their contributions. Let them appreciate how the team works together in getting closer to the goals.

An important tool is a plan sent to all participants that lists forthcoming events and actions, not just meetings, of the process.

An example template for such a plan follows. Following that, I share an instance of people's time being wasted unintentionally.

Process plan (blank)

DATE AND TIME PEOPLE	ACTION / EVENT	FURTHER INFORMATION
Ref. 001		
Ref. 002		
Ref. 003		

Process plan (example)

DATE AND TIME PEOPLE	ACTION / EVENT	FURTHER INFORMATION
Ref. 001 10/03/2024 10.00 AS, GO, DB, DR Meeting room 2, Flamingo House.	Review feed back answers and produce recommendations to be presented at the meeting on 24/03/2024.	A deadline for the return of forms was set for close of business on 22/03/2024.
Ref. 002 10/03/2024 15.00 AS, DR Meeting room 2, Flamingo House	Meeting with contractors to discuss progress on the works on the garden. Report of this meeting to be prepared for the 24/03/2024 meeting.	While work to date has been excellent there is uncertainty over whether some areas are included in the garden and thus in the contract. Hopefully, this meeting will clarify the situation. A site visit to the garden will take place during this meeting.
Ref. 003 12/03/2024 GO	Finalised questionnaire to be uploaded to the web site and tested with a view to going live by 09.00 on 13/03/2024.	The final version has been approved by the officers. The questionnaire closes 10/04/2024. The results to be presented to the April 2024 meeting and a discussion of the findings pencilled in for the May 2024 meeting.

This true example is a warning. A friend who was part of the group campaigning for a community hub in the town complained to me and others that the lottery funding body was biased because it had refused them an important grant.

I contacted the body and it sent me its report. The body had made it clear to the chairperson at the start of the project that funding was unlikely because the building where the hub would be based was not owned by the group. It was a successful shop. The owners had made it clear to the lottery they were not going to sell. The chairperson had never approached the shop.

So why the meetings when the the fate of the project from the start was failure? The chairperson and a couple of others on the group wanted to look important and impress the members, wanting to give the impression that they can get things done. The lessons to be

Chapter 2

TYPES OF MEETINGS

Here is a game to play: one definition of a meeting is where two or more people come together to further a process towards a goal. Create a list of all possible meetings you are involved in. Do this over the next few days. You'll find interesting how many meetings, more informal than formal, there are.

This is a list I made of the various kinds of meetings I attended over one week:

Saying "good morning."	Attending a planning meeting
Taking a parcel to a neighbour.	Meeting a customer
Buying items in a shop.	Asking for advice
Asking for directions	Responding to email
Ordering food and drink in a restaurant	Making and taking phone calls
Making a complaint	Giving a compliment
Attending a family meal	Chairing the local residents' group
Taking my son to the scouts	Attending a doctor's appointment

We consider something as simple as making a purchase in a shop or cafe as a meeting. A good salesperson will seek your custom again. What about wishing a neighbour good morning? We can consider this being a meeting with the purpose of promoting social wellbeing.

When you think about it, you can expand the list and give your own examples.

The most common type of meeting is when people gather in a room at a set date and time for a discussion.

There are other types.

Such as group messages on social media using apps like Facebook Messenger or simply sending email messages back and forth between several people. These are considered meetings, even without a set time.

The weakness of these is having little opportunity for live group discussion and lack of body language. We should not see messaging as an alternative to holding a physical meeting. Although, it can be useful for reporting actions and making requests between meetings as part of the process.

A further problem is that no-one knows how secure or how confidential their messages are. Leaks are possible. Public bodies can have messages revealed to a wider audience because of freedom of information requests.

Under the right circumstances, video conferencing can be a valuable meeting tool. Although not a perfect substitution for meeting in person, it is useful where participants are too far apart. Security issues need to be looked at. A risk assessment that considers the probability of a security breach against the meeting's sensitivity is necessary.

Webinars are good presentation tools where many participants need to get and understand information. Although feedback is low and there is hardly any group discussion, it is a useful way of presenting information.

Online activities like those above can be useful in some circumstances. Make sure that contact information, especially passwords, is secure. In its early days, a lot of bad press for the video platform Zoom, for example, was because participants publicised log in details (sometimes on social media) rather than problems with the app itself.

Chapter 3

EFFECTIVE MEETINGS

What is the ideal length of a productive meeting? Duration varies based on participants, purpose, and time of day. Many meetings can end in 30 minutes or fewer. After about an hour, interest flags. Most meetings shouldn't exceed two hours without a break.

If a meeting needs to be longer, split it with brief breaks and varied activities. Pay attention to the flow so that a break comes at a natural stop. Recaps in long meetings help keep things on track.

I knew a group that used to have subcommittee meetings that went on for about 3 to 4 hours. Mainly because the chair of that subcommittee liked to show how important he believed he was. He did this by using officious phrases, long sentences with unnecessary repeated words and bringing in up to date news he had just looked at that had little or nothing to do with the subject. Designed to impress, such behaviour these days results in poor opinion.

As a result, very few attendees had the opportunity to take part in discussion. Eventually the group decided to end the subcommittees. In this case, the work still got done and in a lot less time. Subcommittees only work if they are run properly and are helpful to the main committee.

Keep the number of participants as low as possible. A dozen seems to be a good maximum. Fewer attendees can cause a quorum shortage or biased decision-making. Too many, results in conflicts and lengthy discussions, making it harder to reach an agreement.

The arrangement for seating is important. The chairperson and their supporters (such as presenters) should sit where they have a clear view of everyone and vice versa.

Participants with disabilities will need appropriate seating and arrangements. For large premises and gatherings, a microphone is essential.

If there are to be any presentations, all attendees should be able to see and hear them clearly. Maybe the seating is rearranged for that part of the meeting.

Chairs should be comfortable for the entire meeting.

I once attended an infant school governors' meeting where we sat on children's chairs. Luckily the meeting was only about half an hour. We could not have remained seated must longer.

When arranging seats, consider distractions. The main two being sunlight and noisy work elsewhere in the building. Make sure blinds are available and seating avoids direct sunshine.

If possible, the organiser should reschedule the meeting for a quieter time or halt the noisy work for the duration of the meeting.

The room should be comfortable. Aim for a comfortable temperature of 20 to 23 Celsius, without excessive humidity.

Most meetings should be formal, although not too formal unless required. A bit of light relief now and then keeps the participants interested.

The agenda lists items for discussion. It is an important document, for without it, the meeting will wander and run out of time. During the early part of the meeting, people will interrupt to ensure they make their points quickly because of the lack of agenda.

A well-prepared agenda makes the meeting more productive.

While a good agenda covers all topics, it is brief. It is dynamic and avoids being too vague or too detailed. The headings should be clear about the point for discussion, for example: "location of our new building" rather than "premises update" to avoid a discussion that misses important points. Avoid headings that are so detailed they stifle discussion.

Participants can suggest agenda topics to the secretary or chairperson in advance. If the chairperson rejects the request, they may need to explain why.

The facilitator excludes topics of interest to only a few on the agenda. Perhaps those few can hold their own separate meeting for that topic.

The agenda should list presenters and durations for each topic to be efficient. It should state whether the item is for noting (just for information), discussion, or requires action. Items for information and not discussion need not be on the agenda. The facilitator can send those in a separate document.

The agenda should clarify if the public is invited for the entire meeting or just certain items. This includes observers, while the status of co-opted members also has to be considered.

Here is an example of an agenda:

WELLS COUNTY NEWSTART PROGRAMME LTD

Chair: Carlton Chambers, Secretary: Glynis A. Wells

City Hall, Strawberry Way, Womenston

Planning Meeting 24 November 7pm - Agenda

Introductions

Apologies

Minutes of the last meeting (15 September)

    3.1 Accuracy of the minutes

    3.2 Any matters arising

4. Correspondence received.

5. To note a verbal report from the membership secretary

6. To discuss the reports (attached) of the working groups:

    6.1 Introducing an improved shopping experience;

    6.2 Examining the needs of young adults and families;

    6.3 Enhancing the visitor experience.

    Each report is limited to thirty minute discussion.

7. Preparation for the Mayor's visit.

8. Any Other Business.

The next planning meeting is scheduled for 17 January 7pm at City Hall. The date of the meeting with the Mayor, which will be in December, is still to be announced.

An agenda usually starts with apologies from those unable to attend. Then the chairperson asks attendees to approve the minutes of the previous meeting as an accurate record. The chair signs a copy to show this is so. The secretary makes any corrections before the chair signs.

Then follows matters arising from those minutes. I've heard of meetings where this has led to discussions that took up most of the meeting. Matters arising should only be a few minutes. Its purpose is to give a brief update on matters discussed at the last meeting that aren't on the agenda of this one. There should be no discussion on the matters. If there needs to be any, the chairperson adds them to the agenda of the meeting if urgent, or to the agenda of the next if not.

Importantly, members should not decide on matters arising that are not on the distributed agenda. Here is an important example of how a group of school governors went against this. They voted to convert to an academy during a discussion on matters arising. It wasn't an agenda item. It annoyed governors not present. If they had known a vote was to be taken, they would have made arrangements to attend.

Items such as correspondence and reports from other meetings should not take up much time to avoid rushing major subjects on the agenda.

Having an agenda means participants are aware of the subjects to be discussed and when. An excellent idea is for it to be a timetable too, although the chair needs to be aware when it is important for an item to run over. A timetable, however, gives a reason for the chair to stop time consuming irrelevant talk. It's important that all participants are aware of the timetable and help to stick to it.

An important item should be on the agenda as early as possible so that there is plenty of time to discuss it while attention before attention flags.

Contact information should be on the agenda so members know whom to contact should they need to suggest something for the agenda, give apologies or be late. It should give the names and positions of participants for the benefit of all participants.

"Any Other Business" is usually for announcements not covered by the meeting. As with "Matters Arising" participants should not use it for discussion or resolutions. They can ask for such things to be added to the next agenda. Urgent items should have been to the chair's notice at the start of the meeting to be added to the agenda, rather than under "any other business."

The last item on the agenda should be the time and place of the next meeting. This keeps the chain of meetings connected. One reason groups fold is because at the end, participants don't know when the next meeting will be.

While we should avoid late changes to the agenda (participants have only prepared for the items listed) sometimes making one is necessary.

Before starting each item, it's useful for the chair to summarise what the item is about and why it's on the agenda.

Where the meeting is virtual, the notice sent with the agenda should give the video platform and explain where participants can get advice on using that platform and technical help. Where such a meeting is international or in a large country, give the time zone of the start time.

To avoid eyestrain, virtual meetings should not be too long.

As well as speaking, participants should also engage in active listening. This is important, as it's a key component for them to work together. A good way to improve active listening is to hold a brainstorming session.

Training is important. Such as using an external provider for teaching better communications or team-building exercises.

A good rule for people to take part and contribute is avoid interruptions, criticism of a person rather than the action, disclosure of private information and allegations without proof.

Technology to improve meetings has improved over the years, more so in recent times. The main ones are:

Projection onto a screen, whiteboards, microphone and speaker systems, video linking, conference phones, computers and printers.

Technology is good when it works, but irritating when it doesn't, so have a Plan B. For each of the list above, I explain its usefulness and an alternative should any don't work properly.

Projectors allow information to be seen by a wide audience. If it fails, or the computer feeding it fails, there is a problem. Arrange for backup equipment to be available and transfer presentations, such as PowerPoint slides, to the new equipment. You might need to download software from a cloud, so make sure you understand the venue's Wi-Fi, including access to any password needed. As a last resort, get the presentation slides printed for distribution.

Microphones are very useful for helping participants to hear. Even a moderately sized venue microphones are useful. Also, consider loop systems for to assist those with hearing aids, consider hiring a sign language interpreter if there are those in the audience who require one.

For video linking and conference phones, which allow participation by those who cannot access the meeting in person, have a backup system ready. Most Internet video services have the facility to take part by phone if needed.

Whiteboards allow the presenter to get information, especially visual information, across clearly. Make sure the markers won't run out and that they will write clearly. You could use a flip chart as a backup.

If you're producing printed documents for distribution, have a spare cartridge ready.

Reporting progress is a key factor of meetings that seek to find and implement solutions.

Deadlines are important. Monitoring of each deadline is as well.

We should normally avoid holding meetings at short notice (attendees have to rearrange diaries, cannot attend, and it can increase stress resulting in a departure from the mission). One might have to be held as an emergency measure.

What is the problem exactly? What is the cause? Why is it a problem? This process takes time, so an emergency meeting while dealing with the urgent matter will need to be backed up by a later meeting as part of a process to prevent a reoccurrence of the meeting.

After members have found the problem, the next stage is to look for potential solutions (using methods such as brainstorming), exploring the advantages and disadvantages of each. Members then implement and evaluate at least one of the chosen solutions.

There are ways of finding solutions to problems. The following steps create a helpful plan.

1. Root cause analysis. Decide what the problem is. Ask why it is a problem and then ask why the answer is a problem. Members keep asking until they discover the root cause.

What is the problem?

A key component failed.

Why did it fail?

A nut became unscrewed.

Why did it unscrew?

The process causes vibrations that causes the nut to slowly turn.

Why does it slowly turn?

Over time the nut wears and no longer fits perfectly.

2. Consider workable solutions. In this example, a short-term solution is to replace the nut more often. A long-term one is to find a more durable replacement for the screw and its nut.

3. Evaluate the solutions. Look at both positive and negative aspects. Cost will usually be a negative one, but the aim is to overcome the problem. It's a matter of balancing the positives and negatives.

4. Test the solution in a trial.

5. Evaluate the trial.

6. If successful, go ahead with the solution. If not, return to step 2 or 3.

Effective meetings are important to this process. If we don't hold proper meetings, wrong decisions and imperfect solutions will not cause the problem to be solved.

\

Chapter 4

BEING EFFECTIVE AT MEETINGS

If you aren't the chairperson, sit as close to the chairperson as possible. This makes you look important, and you'll find you can view the meeting better.

Help the Chair conduct the meeting. Help them deal with difficult attendees.

At meetings, control your emotions and try to show empathy with others. An occasional argument can clear the air, but staying calm and understanding the other person's point of view is usually beneficial. Focus on the action rather than the person.

Start by active listening. Pay attention and avoid interrupting. Don't hesitate to seek clarification if you want this.

When speaking, keep your speeches concise and clear.

Use story telling as a way of making your speeches interesting. Back up visions or statistics with personal stories. People prefer to hear stories rather than boring sentences. Story telling done right engages your audience to such as extent that they feel inspired.

Start your story with a beginning (the problem) then a middle (the actions taken) and finally an ending that shows the solution to the problem. Make your audience emotionally involved in the story somehow. Emphasise the conflict and the resolution. End with a memorable phrase.

Body language is important. Keep eye contact with each of your audience. Keep them engaged, make them wonder what's coming next. Control your tone and pace of voice to be an excellent storyteller.

Remember to pay attention to your body language at all times in the meeting, not just when telling a story, to help get your point across. Greet with a firm handshake, keep good eye contact, have open gestures, smile and avoid touching your face. Keep your head up.

Look at the camera, not the screen, during a video conference.

Manage your time by concentrating on priorities and updating your diary as soon as possible.

Use delegation and motivating words to encourage others to do work so you're not doing everything. Show that you and others are part of the same team.

Pay attention to the saying: under promise and over deliver.

Networking is important to find others who can help you and the team. Opportunities for networking can spring up suddenly so, always have your networking tools (pen, notebook and business cards) with you.

Chapter 5

THE ADMINISTRATOR

This is typically called the secretary. Their role includes note taking, dealing with correspondence and (under guidance from the chairperson) assisting participants with the process.

The chairperson and facilitator's collaboration is important for meeting success and goal achievement.

Ahead of the meeting, the administrator sends participants documents, including the agenda. Take extra copies to the meeting in case anyone forgets theirs. Carrying spare pens and any other requirements is another good idea.

The header on all correspondence from the group, especially the agenda, should include the administrator's contact details.

The administrator works with the chairperson to plan meetings and get and organise useful information.

Ideally, the administrator should not be a participant, as it is difficult to concentrate on making accurate notes and taking part in the meeting. An excellent administrator is too busy listening to talk. Let a participant take the role if necessary. In that case, it may be useful to rotate the role between participants from one meeting to the next.

Here's an idea for a chairperson where one person unduly dominates the meeting: ask that person to be the administrator if the meeting needs one. It's hard to take notes and selfishly talk throughout the meeting.

Presenters can help the administrator by giving them a copy of their notes and visual aids.

The chairperson and secretary work together to create reliable draft minutes. However, it is for all participants to approve the minutes as an accurate record at the next meeting.

"Accuracy of the minutes" is an agenda item where the chair asks if the draft minutes are an accurate record. A person present at the meeting moves this and, after a seconder, members vote on the accuracy of the minutes. This item is not the same as "matters arising from the minutes," which is usually the next one.

"Matters arising" is for brief updates on items that are not on the agenda. For discussions or urgent decisions about any update, add the item to the current or next meeting agenda.

Some administrators would like to make a sound recording for making accurate minutes. However, be aware that some might not feel comfortable saying something that is recorded. Not that they are lying, but because they are concerned about someone using it out of context. Promising to erase the tape after the secretary has written the minutes might help. However, for ease of mind, we should avoid sound recording if not needed.

Using the administrator as the point of contact is an affective action. Never assume that the chairperson is the only one who decides and others ignored.

Where the chairperson is not up to the required standard, it falls upon the administrator to keep the meeting focussed on the agenda and its timetable.

When producing the minutes, do so in a standard way so that all can follow them with ease. To help with this, the template includes standard headings that follow the agenda and a numbering system for paragraphs. Easy for someone to refer to point 3.1, for example, rather than "the second paragraph on page 2."

However, change the template if participants consider this is improves the minutes.

Chapter 6

THE IMPORTANCE OF THE CHAIRPERSON

This is the most important role. The Chairperson doesn't just control the meeting; they are usually in charge of the complete process.

A good chairperson avoids dominating the conversation. They do not control the meeting to their own satisfaction rather than the group's. Such actions turn attendees into a passive audience. Interest declines and membership decreases.

To avoid arguments, participants should talk (especially during debates) to the Chair rather than address each other. The Chair's role is to see that the meeting moves forward with everyone taking part and feeling involved.

The Chair's roles may be general, but there are different chairing styles. The actual style depends on the process itself.

An excellent chairperson ensures everyone contributes, even the unsure. No-one needs to feel neglected.

For example, the chairperson could ask: "do you have anything to say about that opinion?" or, "you haven't spoken yet, do you have a strong view about this topic?" Asking closed questions like these brings the opportunity to contribute or say "no." If the latter, the person feels valued even when they don't wish to comment.

To prevent anyone from feeling singled out, the chairperson can ask each participant if they have anything to add at the end of the discussion or meeting.

The chairperson ensures a smooth flow of the meeting and encourages all to contribute. They say little during the meeting, mostly words to keep the meeting going. They sum up what was said and decided. The chairperson ensures participants understand the proposal before voting.

It is important that the chairperson has the means to control the meeting. They should be seen and heard by all, have a microphone and gavel if needed. Hopefully, they will never or rarely use the gavel.

The chairperson can interrupt the flow of a participant if that person is upsetting the meeting, e.g. the speech is going over the allotted time or the participant is using unacceptable language.

The chairperson should vacate the chair in favour of the vice-chairperson if they want to participate in the discussion extensively.

He sees that the meeting does not go on too long, that members keep interested and that no one dominates the meeting. All participants, with the help of the chairperson, must address any rudeness or trouble and ensure everyone stays focused on the agenda.

The chairperson should know which items are urgent and which are important.

I have been to meetings where someone heard a word that reminded them of a story to tell. The story had no relevance. It led to others joining in a discussion that had nothing to do with the meeting's purpose.

Another problem is participants discussing a topic for longer than the allocated time. To move forward, reschedule the item to a longer time or form a subgroup that discusses and reports.

The chairperson begins the meeting by outlining the project, its purpose and meeting objectives. This focuses participants from the start.

To achieve good flow, participants should understand each other. For example, asking a participant to explain a technical term or slang phrase that others may not be familiar with. (There's a glossary explains key word in this book at the end.)

Group bias occurs when a group holds a strong belief that disregards opposing information and opinions. it accepts supporting opinions without question.

Such a bias needs to be challenged to test its validity. In order to achieve this, we should encourage participants to express their views with no worry that others might disagree.

In formal meetings, there may be a vote. Although we prefer a consensus, the rules usually require holding a vote where this does not happen. It's important to know who can vote and that those who can't don't. Observers and guests (such as a councillor invited to a residents' group for advice) rarely have a vote.

The chairperson can vote. They're on the committee, after all. Although, they may decide to abstain, having the view that to vote tempts the losing side to accuse them of having a bias throughout.

In the event of a tie, the chairperson has a second vote. It is customary, although not binding, that this vote is used to keep the status quo, the present situation.

Once the meeting has voted, everyone should accept the decision. As the saying goes, "that's democracy."

It is better to tackle an issue rather than leave it unresolved. Eventually, it will have to be tackled. The sooner it is, the better.

When conflicts arise, the chairperson can meet with those involved outside the meeting to discuss and resolve them. Chairpersons should be good at conflict management. The best chairperson sets a good example.

Where the chairperson expects disagreements they can start with areas of agreement to make progress before addressing disagreements.

The chairperson shouldn't do everything. They should be at ease delegating while keeping overall control.

The chairperson should gather feedback from participants after the meeting. This helps to improve the next meeting.

Although the administrator handles activities like messages and emails between meetings, it is essential that the chairperson keeps a calendar. The chairperson needs to be aware of what is going on and when. The calendar can be any form they prefer.

The calendar needs to record the key people with the event. The chairperson sees the event and the people involved.

It is useful for the chairperson to have the contact details of key people in case the administrator is not available.

Organisations require officers like a chair, secretary, and treasurer, but other positions can also contribute. These are officers for specific functions such as membership recruitment and retention, engagement with particular groups of members (for example, new members) and external communication and publicity.

These are functions that a subgroup can administer rather than one officer if needed.

However, a capable and enthusiastic member is an excellent opportunity for this role. Having, for example, a membership or youth officer doesn't excuse others from doing their share of the work. All positions require support from other members.

Chapter 7

TAKING NOTES

Notes should record what points participants make and, most important, what actions the group decides and by whom.

Avoid excessive detail in the minutes or notes. Avoid pronouns such as "he said." Make sure anyone reading the notes knows the role of attendees.

The minutes produced from the notes have two purposes.

The first, to provide an excellent meeting record. Once accepted as an accurate record, the minutes provide evidence of how the meeting proceeded. This could be a legal requirement. Others can consider that an action not minuted did not take place.

The minutes give the title of the meeting, its date, a list of those attending, and a list of those who were asked to attend and have given apologies.

The note taker must understand the purpose of the meeting and its part in the overall process.

The note taker should know about the participants' expertise. Perhaps, not as much detailed knowledge, but enough knowledge to understand the process.

The chairperson needs the note taker to have clarity of the process before and after the meeting. To help, a note taker should consider taking a course.

It is important that whenever required within the meeting, the note taker asks for clarity. This could be to make sure what actions are agreed or, with a proposed motion, what its wording is. The latter is important where the meeting has amended a motion.

The note taker needs to make an accurate and clear list of actions naming who handles them.

The secretary should store the minutes where others can find them. Officers should know how to get past minutes easily. Officers should check the past minutes so that matters dealt with are not being revisited unnecessarily. Viewing past minutes is recommended for new participants to be informed.

Chapter 8

PRESENTERS AND EXPERTS

The inclusion and timing of handouts should complement your presentation. Before the meeting is useful so that participants can prepare, particularly if they need to understand concepts in order to appreciate your presentation.

At the start can be problematic unless they complement your presentation. Otherwise, participants may be more interested in studying the handout rather than listening to your words.

The end of your presentation is the time to provide a summary and give further sources of information.

Practice your presentation beforehand, not just to yourself. Friends and family can help with advising on matters such as timing, flow and interest. Make sure you can deliver your presentation within your time spot.

Others, such as the chairperson, may give the duration, or it may be within your gift. If the latter, consider what reasonable length of time your audience would prefer. To avoid rushing at the end, spoiling your summing up, aim to be shorter than the actual time.

Be prepared for obvious questions. If you cannot put them in your presentation, have the answers prepared. Be aware that you can't anticipate every question. If you can't answer any questions, be honest and promise to provide the answer later.

Agree with meeting facilitator what you will need. Ensure all equipment, including the digital projector, is functional before the meeting and prior to your presentation.

Sign in at reception, then find your seat and presentation spot in the room.

Before you deliver the presentation, check the room and where the audience is sitting.

During your presentation keep eye contact, always use a microphone if provided even if you think you don't need it. Projectors can be noisy. Turn these off when you don't need them, especially while you are talking.

Interact with the audience rather than just lecture. A metaphor - people prefer to watch a movie than attend most lectures. Why? Because movies entertain them.

Watch your pace and give clues when you are about to finish. If you suggest you are about to finish, do not carry on. The audience will expect you to finish.

Here are some tips:

focus on those people listening to you

 interact with them

ask them questions

do a poll of their opinions

praise their responses.

Use humour by all means, but be careful. Humour works well if it's appropriate and that comes about by knowing your audience and loving your subject.

Be honest, be yourself, be truthful. People are skilled at spotting insincerity and deceit, even when they pretend otherwise to be polite. Be relaxed. Nearly everyone is on your side.

If you make a mistake, carry on. People are listening because they are interested in your message, not to judge you.

Avoid reading a speech word for word. Where is the interaction with that? Memorise the basics of your message for a good delivery. Your audience will understand you far better than listening to pre-written words.

Use slides effectively. They should enhance the impact of your words, not detract from them. You and your slide presentation are a double act. If the audience can understand everything from your slides, what are you there for?

Be aware if there are interpreters, including those of sign languages present. You will need to help them by making sure they can clearly hear you and are not speaking too fast.

Finish both your presentation and your last answer with something memorable that's suggested by the topic. Something emotional. It can be a joke, an interesting fact, an anecdote, or a challenge.

Answer questions efficiently and as briefly as possible. I have heard presenters frequently spend ages answering a question, particularly one they know the answer to, meandering onto other points. They hope this tactic with lessen the number of questions within the time slot so, reducing the chance of being asked that embarrassing question. It's not a good tactic. Long irrelevant answers can bore the audience rather than entertain them.

If you hear a question but others do not, you can repeat the question to everyone. This is better than asking the member to repeat their question.

Stay in your position until the chairperson signals you can sit back down.

If you have to leave after your presentation, that can be fine. Participants, however, may appreciate you if you stay, particularly if they wish to talk to you afterwards.

Chapter 9

MONEY MATTERS

The word "treasurer" can be enough to put people off the role. There is the view that once taken, no one else with take over.

Well, let's calm down. The role is less daunting than people think. For this role, we need someone skilled in figures and spreadsheets. While the treasurer banks the money and keeps the accounts, the committee is responsible for monitoring the flow of money. If the treasurer does take the club's money to South America, it's everyone's fault, not just the greedy person. Keeping the accounts for companies, large and medium, may mean paying an accountant and buying a reliable software package like Sage®. Small groups, however, do not have to go that expense as a simple cash book or basic spreadsheet software can satisfy the group's financial recording needs.

The financial records should be as simple as needed. The finances should provide a clear narrative of income, expenses, and future projections. In order to do this cash flow prediction with some accuracy, it is important the group keep the accounts up to date.

The treasurer should file and reference documents efficiently. Simple actions, such as writing cheque numbers on receipts, is a good practice. On a visit to a shop, buy items for the group separately from those for personal use. That way, the receipt presented is clear for an auditor to follow.

Note the date, source, and amount of incomes and the date, amount, and reason of payments. All that's required is a basic running total that adds income and subtracts expenditure.

Bank money and cheques as soon as possible. Why? First and foremost, to prevent the transaction from being forgotten. Suddenly discovering a stash of ten-pound notes that someone should have banked a few months ago is embarrassing. Even more so if it's because someone says at the AGM, "hold on a minute, what happened to that raffle money we raised?"

That reminds me: look out for those foreign coins and old pound coins that still turn up in collections.

Banking money straightaway makes sure the group gains maximum interest on the money. Anyone can bank the money, it needn't be the treasurer. However, inform the treasurer so the books are up to date and correct.

Accounts should clearly distinguish between restricted and unrestricted funds. The latter is money raised, such as membership fees and raffle income, for no specific purpose. The former is income raised for a specific project. Grants usually come under the former. The membership should be aware of the funding allocated for specific projects.

It is a good practice to include diagrams, such as linear, bar and pie charts, when presenting information.

This chart is linear:

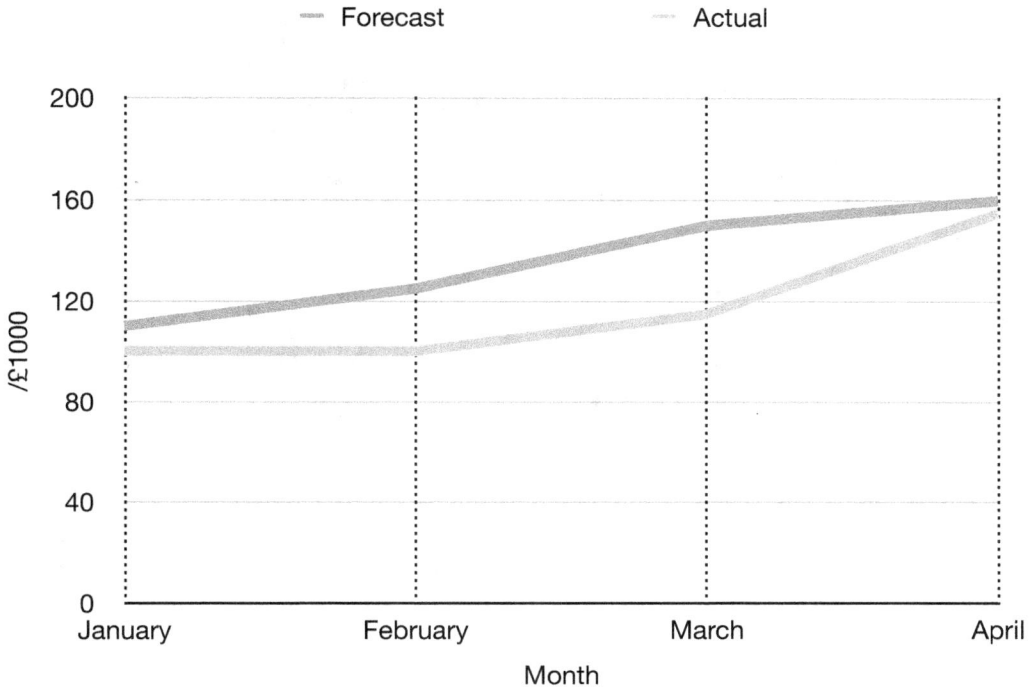

Forecast Income v Actual Income

A bar chart example:

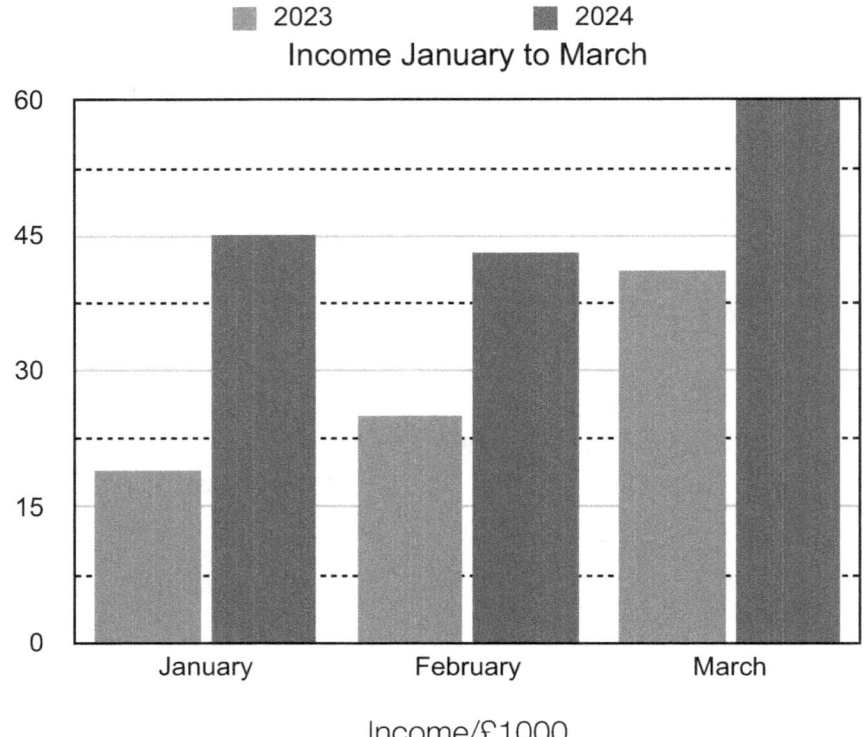

A pi chart example:

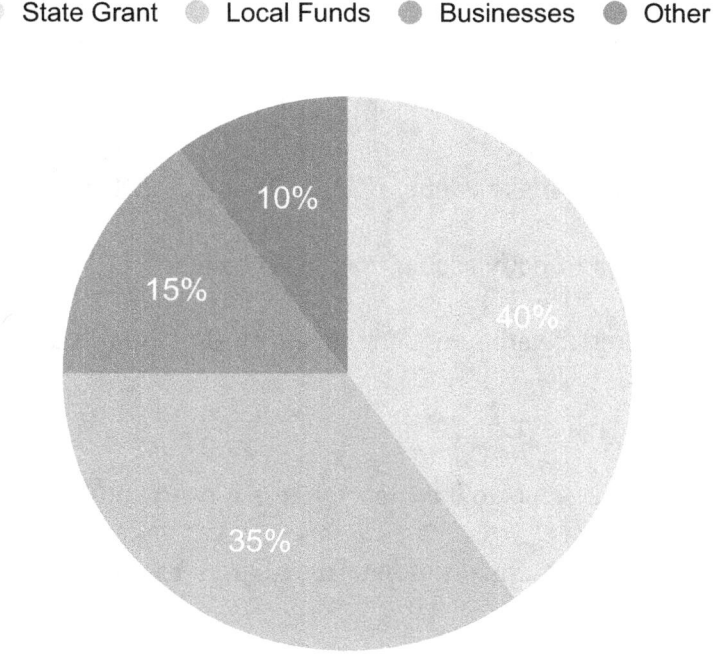

State Grant   Local Funds   Businesses   Other

Sources of income January to April

One group met monthly and paid the venue by cheque each month for use of the room. One year, one person asked at the AGM why weren't twelve room hire transactions in the annual account. Sometimes it was eleven, sometimes thirteen. Can you think why?

Well, the transactions recorded the number of times in the financial year the cheques were cashed. If one written in the financial year was cashed after the year end, it would show up in the next year's account rather than this year's.

Try to keep the financial reports in line with the aims and objectives. That way, the group gets an idea of the relative costs of the aims.

All members should be aware that the accounts involve everyone, not just the treasurer.

Everyone should know the financial situation. Someone should be able to take over quickly if the treasurer becomes indisposed.

All members should help the treasurer. If using bank bags, place the correct amount of coins in each bag, checking them to make sure they are correct.

Income that isn't banked should not be used for payments. To do so, results in the accounts not fitting with the bank account. It makes analysis of the sources of income difficult and inaccurate. "Did we really only make twenty pounds from the raffle when we sold a hundred pounds worth of tickets?" Use a petty cash system with a record.

A receipt explaining the time, the amount, and the reason should replace all money taken from petty cash.

Avoid using personal bank accounts to buy items unless it is urgent. No large amount of spending should occur unless the organisation or meeting gives prior approval, preferably minuted.

The group should find a person or group to audit the accounts. For small groups, this doesn't require a qualified person. Just someone who is independent and trusted to audit the accounts efficiently. For larger organisations with more complicated finances, engage a suitably qualified person.

Chapter 10

CONSTITUTIONS, ANNUAL MEETINGS AND PUBLIC MEETINGS

One residents' meeting was discussing using a gift of a few hundred pounds to pay for a clean up of a riverside that wasn't in the residents' area. Although many opposed this, the chairperson was clearly not impartial and was siding with those for the scheme. So, to curtail the lengthy discussion few wanted, I asked, "it is in the aims of our constitution?" To our surprise, the chairperson told us he hadn't read our constitution. The answer was, it wasn't.

Why do you meet? What are the specific purposes of those invited to your meeting? If you are a group, such as a residents' group, you need a constitution. It is your group's most important document, explaining what your aims and objectives are and providing rules. It is there to give the group focus and to sort out potential conflicts resulting from misunderstandings

The constitution explains the aims and objectives of your group, and how you elect the committee and officers.

Your group could have a mission statement. Although it does not have to, it is an excellent idea. This is a bold statement in one sentence of what your group strives to achieve. It could be a simple one like "to improve our local park." However, a more optimistic mission like "to make our park an enjoyable destination for all our residents and visitors" has more impact.

Your group's name and mission statement should go together. Sometimes, it's better to decide on your group's name after working out your mission statement.

The aims in the constitution explain what your group is about; the actions it wants to achieve. Don't make the list long. Three or four aims at the most. Examples of aims are "to keep our streets clear of litter" and "to find funding for activities for young adults." The aims are important because everything decided at meetings must be under those aims. The chairperson reminds members of the constitution.

We can also specify objectives in the constitution. These are statements that describe the actions that work towards the aims.

Who are the officers? The chairperson and treasurer are important. If possible, there should also be an administrator/secretary and vice chair.

The constitution could also clarify when and how meetings are called. To be flexible, it's better that it mentions a minimum number of meetings rather than a set amount.

For groups, there will have to be a yearly meeting called the Annual General Meeting (AGM). The facilitator invites members to elect officers, and be updated about progress and finances.

I've witnessed a few committees who think they are the group. They aren't. Each committee is answerable to the membership. A residents' group, for example, is answerable to all the residents in the area.

The constitution must have a dissolution clause. This explains how the group ends and what happens to remaining funds. Neither the chair nor the committee can end the group on a whim. The dissolution process must occur as stated in the constitution. This often calls for a special meeting of all members to discuss the dissolution.

A draft constitution follows.

Constitution of (group name)

Name and mission statement of the group.
The aims of the group in a numbered order.
The objectives of group ordered to reflect the order of the aims.
Who can join the group. Usually it is anyone who supports the aims. It's important here that there will be no discrimination and that the group won't tolerate any such discrimination.
The rules for the annual meeting (AGM) usually
That there is a minimum notice of the AGM

That it must be held within, say, fifteen months of the previous AGM.

that outgoing officers give a report on their work during the past year,

That the treasurer give a finance report for the past year including a balance sheet.

Discuss the finances and the membership fee, if any, for the coming year.

Decide on any changes to the constitution, provided the notice included the propose changes. It should detail how the vote is conducted and the number required for a change. Although most organisations stipulate a basic over fifty percent vote in favour, some stipulate a two-thirds majority is required.

Election of the officers and the committee including how they are elected.

Decide on any changes to the signatories of the bank account and who should audit the financial accounts for the coming year.

A general discussion, notice of the subject having been given in he notice.

 (The AGM is not a committee meeting so any matters not relating to the business of the AGM need not be discussed. However, it may be useful as many members are present to have a committee meeting afterwards. Another useful addition is to have a guest speaker whom the members would like to hear and talk to).
The number, if any, of other general meetings including how they are called.

Financial matters such as signatories, banking instructions, and auditing of the accounts,

What happens should the group fold, including where any spare money goes.

Constituted groups hold an annual general meeting (AGM.) It's the opportunity for all members to come together to elect the officers and committee members for the coming year, and to accept the annual financial accounts. Other items on the agenda could include the outgoing chairperson reviewing the year, and deciding future venues and dates.

The AGM is the meeting to decide about changes to the constitution. Consult the constitution for the procedure. The secretary should list any proposed changes in the agenda.

An example of an AGM agenda follows.

OLD LODGE COMPANY

NOTICE IF ANNUAL GENERAL MEETING

12 March 2025 2pm

Manston Centre

AGENDA

1. Welcome and Introduction

2. Minutes of the last AGM

3. Review of the Year

4. Election of Officers

    4.1 Chairperson

    4.2 Vice-Chairperson

    4.3 Secretary

    4.4 Treasurer

5. Election of other committee members

6. Proposed changes to the Constitution

    6.1 Paragraph 15.1 to add "at least" in front of "fifteen pounds."

7. Dates and venues of future ordinary meetings.

8. Date and venue of next year's AGM

9. Guest speaker (Martin Glane, CEO of Queen's Bridge Parade.)

The AGM is a general meeting for all qualifying individuals. A residents' group, for example, should invite all residents in its designated area. The constitution should specify who can attend a general meeting. It should outline the procedure for calling and publicising a general meeting.

One major question for AGMs is: who chairs the meeting given that the election of the chairperson is one of the agenda items?

There are two ways forward. The chairperson resigns first and hands over the chairing to the vice-chairperson. The new or re-elected chairperson then takes charge of the meeting. The other option is to invite a trusted outsider, like the mayor or a councillor, to chair the AGM. The election of other officers then proceeds. Participants nominate and a vote taken. The constitution might stipulate secret ballots. If not, it's usually a show of hands unless the meeting decides on secret ballots.

Here's a note about public meetings that exclude public participation.

It's important for the public to observe but refrain from interfering with the meeting. Where an interference arises, the chairperson deals with it immediately and firmly. If it continues, the meeting will need to be paused, stopped, or continued in private.

One meeting held in public was interrupted by a member of the public who repeatedly shouted that the committee was corrupt. He ignored all requests to be quiet because he had a hidden agenda. He wanted to make the news of being thrown out for his views. He had tipped off the press. It didn't work because the chairperson moved the meeting to private session. As a result, the protester was not popular with other members of the public who wanted to watch the meeting.

Public meetings where the public takes part can be problematic. As an alternative, hold a drop-in session where members talk one-on-one with the public. If it has to be a public meeting, the chairperson should emphasise the need for all to be civil and have a chance to speak. Avoid the situation where one person claims to the spokesperson for all but really speaks for themself and others dare not express a different opinion. Encourage each person to air their own view.

Chapter 11

FEEDBACK AND EVALUATION

Meetings can become habits. There are good points and bad points about habits.

Let's start with the good. Once we find a good way of doing things, as we repeat it, it becomes easier to do. For example, booking a room means finding who to contact and how to pay. That's a task. For future meetings, you know who to email or how to book online, you know how to make the payments. Still a task, not a daunting one, because you are just repeating previous actions. It has become a routine, a habit.

After all, practice makes perfect, as do repeated actions.

That's fine then? Well, habits can also become bad ones, especially when we just follow the same routines without asking why or, more importantly, asking if they are still relevant. We don't want the process to stagnate. We don't want it to keep going without a clear objective.

So feedback and evaluation are important.

Ask participants for their thoughts on the meeting shortly after it ends.

Here are some suggested questions:

Was the meeting to your expectations?

Was the meeting chaired properly?

Did you feel like a participant?

Was the meeting about the right length?

Was the meeting important to the mission?

Do you feel you can work okay with the other participants?

Notice these are closed questions, questions requiring a yes or no answer.

You could use evaluation instead. Instead of asking about the meeting's length, rate it on a scale of 0 (to short) to 5 (too long). You could also rate the chair's effectiveness on a scale of 0 to 5. Indeed, using the same scale for all the questions makes the feedback form easy to fill in. You are getting useful information by encouraging as many as possible to give their views.

Also use open questions that require an opinion or observation as an answer. For example, "what did you think of the chairing of the meeting?" or "what is your opinion about the time for questions?"

Feedback doesn't just explain how the meeting went with ideas for improvement, it also gives participants an opportunity to explain the ways they would like to take part in the future.

Feedback forms shouldn't be too long. More than one sheet of A4 may put people off completing them.

Where feedback forms ask for personal details, such as country of birth, for monitoring, keep this part is anonymous. Collect contact details separately for follow up, and informing the participants why. You must use the latest guidance on data protection and GDPR.

You could even get feedback on how you ask for feedback. As any feedback is useful, that's good. All feedback, negative and positive, we consider being helpful. Negative feedback isn't the same as criticism.

GLOSSARY

ABSTAIN

To abstain is to choose not to vote.

ACTION POINT

An item in the minutes that requires action to be taken.

AD HOC MEETING

A meeting held for a particular purpose.

AGENDA

The list of items to be discussed.

AMENDMENT

Minor changes to a motion. An amendment can add to, delete from or change the wording of a motion, but cannot negate the motion.

APOLOGIES

Saying sorry that you are unable to attend the meeting.

BRAINSTORMING

A thorough discussion for expressing ideas and creating solutions.

CARRIED

A motion adopted by the group is said to be carried.

CHAIRPERSON

Someone who presides over a meeting.

CHAIR'S CASTING VOTE

The second vote of the chair should the result be a tie.

COMMITTEE

A group of people appointed or elected to perform a service or function.

CONSTITUTION

The principles of an organisation.

DEFEATED

A motion is defeated if the majority vote against it.

DELEGATE

A person chosen to represent the group at another meeting.

EX OFFICIO

A person who has the right to attend because of their position or office.

FACILITATOR

A person who helps the group or meeting to progress.

FEEDBACK

Information from an inquiry.

MINUTES

An official record of the proceedings of the meeting.

MODEL

An example that could be followed.

MOTION

A proposal to be discussed and voted on.

MOVE CLOSURE

A motion to end the debate and go to the vote.

MOVER

A person who introduces a motion to the meeting.

POINT OF INFORMATION

In debate, to clarify something that is said about a pervious speaker.

POINT OF ORDER

To make a point about the process of the debate

QUORUM

The minimum number of attendees required for a meeting to make decisions.

PROCEDURAL MOTION

A motion about the way the business is conducted.

SECONDER

Someone who supports a motion in order that it is debated.

SMART GOALS

Goals that are specific, measurable, achievable, relevant and time bound.

STANDING ORDERS

Written rules that regulate meetings.

TERMS OF REFERENCE

The scope and limitations of the group or meeting.

FURTHER READING

Running Virtual Meetings (HBR 20-Minute Manager Series): Test Your Technology, Keep Their Attention, Connect Across Time Zones

- Paperback : 112 pages
- ISBN-10 : 9781633691490
- ISBN-13 : 978-1633691490
- Publisher : Harvard Business Review Press (2 Aug. 2016)

The Surprising Science of Meetings: How You Can Lead your Team to Peak Performance by Steven G. Rogelberg

- Hardcover : 192 pages
- ISBN-10 : 0190689218
- ISBN-13 : 978-0190689216
- Publisher : OUP USA (25 April 2019)

The Ladybird Book of the Meeting (Ladybirds for Grown-Ups) by Jason Hazeley and Joel Morris

- Hardcover : 56 pages
- ISBN-13 : 978-0718184377
- ISBN-10 : 0718184378
- Publisher : Michael Joseph; 1st edition (20 Oct. 2016)

HBR Guide to Making Every Meeting Matter (Harvard Business Review Guides)

- Paperback : 144 pages
- ISBN-10 : 1633692175
- ISBN-13 : 978-1633692176
- Publisher : Harvard Business Review Press (6 Dec. 2016)

PS

I trust our meeting has been successful. That you understand how meetings can be

productive, exciting and efficient. That you know what to do about those that are not.

In line what I advise please leave your feedback. This can be done by a rating on Amazon or

Goodreads and leaving a comment. I hope it's positive although any ideas for improvement

are appreciated.

Carlton Chambers

January 2024

wrightandreid.com

www.ingramcontent.com/pod-product-compliance
Lightning Source LLC
Chambersburg PA
CBHW082227290526

45794CB00009B/3705